YC
COMF
ARIES ᵤ₂₃
PERSONAL
HOROSCOPE

Monthly Astrological Prediction Forecast
Readings of Every Zodiac Astrology Sun Star
Signs- Love, Romance, Money, Finances, Career,
Health, Travel, Spirituality.

Iris Quinn

Alpha Zuriel Publishing

Your Complete Aries 2023 Personal Horoscope/ Iris Quinn. --
1st ed.

*We are born at a specific time and place, and,
like vintage years of wine, we have the
characteristics of the year and season in which
we are born. Astrology claims nothing more.*
— CARL JUNG

CONTENTS

CHAPTER ONE

ARIES PROFILE

Constellation: Aries

Zodiac symbol: Ram

Date: March 20 – April 19

Zodiac element: Fire

Zodiac quality: Cardinal

Greatest Compatibility: Leo and Libra

Sign ruler: Mars

Day: Tuesday

Color: Red

Birthstone: Diamond

ARIES TRAITS

- There is no filter.
- Become enraged, then forgets why they are enraged

- They believe that everything is a game that they can win.
- On a dare, they'll do anything.
- Bored easily

PERSONALITY OF ARIES

Aries, at their core, do what they want and do things their way. They are unafraid of controversy, fiercely competitive, truthful, and forthright. An Aries is not burdened by the freedom of choice, and they are arguably the least torn about what they want. They leap into the world with zeal and without reservation. It is one of their most admirable characteristics, but it also costs them a tremendous amount of suffering and grief.

Aries are driven by a need to establish their worth and strength. They take command naturally and are competitive and ambitious. Aries are impulsive and bold.

They are adventurous and enjoy exploring. They are determined and courageous, and they excel at starting new endeavors. They have a lot of enthusiasm and can take action quickly. They can also be impatient, but they have a lot of energy and don't like to waste time.

While Aries enjoy competition, they do not enjoy playing games. They are self-aware, have firm beliefs, and are constantly prepared to defend them.

WEAKNESSES OF ARIES

Aries people are impetuous, impatient, and fiery. They make no apologies for their rage. They truly mean, "I don't care." They don't always have the best self-control; therefore, therefore they need to practice being patient.

Aries, who are addicted to action and excitement, are frequently the source of their own problems. All Aries desire to feel everything deeply, which is why they can be prone to irresponsible risk-taking. It also indicates that they frequently react emotionally rather than rationally.

RELATIONSHIP COMPATIBILITY WITH ARIES

Based only on their Sun signs, this is how Aries interacts with others. These are the compatibility interpretations for all 12 potential Aries combinations. This is a limited and insufficient method of determining compatibility. However, Sun-sign compatibility remains the foundation for overall harmony in a relationship.

The general rule is that yin and yang do not get along. Yin complements yin, and yang complements yang. While yin and yang partnerships can be successful, they require more effort. Earth and water zodiac signs are both Yin. Yang is represented by the fire and air zodiac signs.

Aries and Aries

A love affair between two Aries people is a total explosion. To make this relationship work, one of them must give up first. Aries is a competitive sign. These two will not only compete with one another, but will also debate in order to make their points. Despite the fact that they are both yang energy, there may be too much combustion and energy for a happy union. This isn't a good match unless both of them have other planet placements that make them nicer people.

Taurus and Aries

Aries and Taurus are a yin-yang couple. Taurus' sexuality can unite with Aries' life energy if they both work together to make it happen. In a good relationship, they can complement each other, but they must learn to respect one another's natural differences: Aries is an impetuous, fighter, and action-oriented sign. Taurus is focused and walks slowly but steadily. This is something that can be accomplished with hard work.

Gemini and Aries

There are numerous opportunities for Aries and Gemini to create a stable partnership. They can, however, thrive together with greater security if they both mature. They both place high importance on freedom, independence, and the satisfaction of gratifying their curiosity. The major difference: Aries' faithfulness against Gemini's infidelity. Overall, this is yang energy that is compatible.

Cancer and Aries

Aries and Cancer have a challenging yin-yang relationship. They might be able to fit together with Aries' patience, a lot of patience. However, if they wish to pursue their connection, they must both put forth significant effort. Cancer will think Aries is too self-centered. Every time the unpredictable Aries decides to go out where the action is, Cancer will feel quite apprehensive. Aries, on the other hand, will become frustrated by Cancer's insecurity. This partnership needs a lot of effort.

Leo and Aries

Aries and Leo are like fire and ice, but that doesn't make their partnership impossible. Because both Aries and Leo have strong personalities, there will be moments of huge outburst. Leo must relinquish some control over the relationship. In exchange for relinquishing some control, Leo can enjoy everything Aries does to express love. Aries has no issues as long as it boosts Leo's self-esteem. Aries values the freedom that Leo provides, which grows stronger the more Aries promotes Leo's self-esteem.

Virgo and Aries

This is a difficult relationship to maintain. Both Aries and Virgo have strong personalities, yet their ambitions are totally different. Aries is an action-oriented mindset, whereas Virgo is always analyzing and shredding any situation that happens. Aries has to progress, but Virgo is impeding him with judgments and reprimands. Maybe, with a lot of effort, they'll discover a way.

Libra and Aries

Because they are compatible signs, Aries and Libra can form a strong partnership. The most difficult aspect will be Libra constantly reminding Aries that there is a better way to carry out this or that action. And Aries will always behave without regard for Libra's point of view. To avoid a breakup over this issue, Aries and Libra will need to appeal to their tolerance for each other's ways. Aries and Libra are on opposite sides of the same axis and must meet in the middle.

Scorpio and Aries

A partnership between Aries and Scorpio will quickly become difficult. Physical intimacy is the best common ground for these two to understand each other. They are, nonetheless, profoundly different in their ways of thinking and feeling. Scorpio desires complete control over the relationship and its partner, but Aries is unwilling to give it up. They are best suited to an occasional relationship.

Sagittarius and Aries

Aries and Sagittarius can have a wonderful partnership. Sagittarius will assist Aries in learning how to let go of the continual obligations and responsibilities that drag it down. In turn, Aries will assist Sagittarius in channeling its life with increased responsibility. They will have a long-lasting connection if they proceed slowly.

Capricorn and Aries

Aries and Capricorn 0have an extremely difficult relationship. Their personalities are too dissimilar to complement one another harmoniously. Aries acts on impulse without forethought, whereas Capricorn meticulously plans before taking action. Capricorn's continual criticism will not be tolerated by Aries.

Capricorn's tone is too authoritative for Aries. Capricorn, on the other hand, will have a tough time supporting Aries' style of life, which Capricorn regards as silly.

Aquarius and Aries

A connection between Aries and Aquarius might be fruitful. Both members must be patient. Both Aries and Aquarius crave freedom and independence. They will understand each other better as a result of this. The troubles will stem from Aries' hasty and sudden actions, whereas Aquarius requires more time and security before moving on anything.

Pisces and Aries

Pisces is too introspective and ethereal for Aries, who is a fire sign that meets life head on. Aries represents a risk that Pisces does not believe they are willing to take. Pisces requires security and tranquility to develop and prosper. These are characteristics that Aries rarely exhibits. Aries must control their impulses in order for this relationship to work.

LOVE AND PASSION

When it comes to conquering someone, Aries is primitive. Aries men and women enjoy taking the initiative. Men to demonstrate their masculinity, and women to demonstrate their attractiveness. Because of this, some of their adventures don't go past the initial excitement and mystery of the conquest and end quickly.

When an Aries fully falls in love, there is no room for compromise. They are romantic idealists at heart, and they will do anything to keep the love alive.

Some people are overly optimistic, while others are unable to look past their own ambitions and demands.

Aries need to express themselves physically. They understand how to truly enjoy sexuality. In this area, both men and women born under the sign of Aries are very active and quick to act, but they can also be too demanding at times.

MARRIAGE

To keep an Aries happy in a relationship, their partner must keep the connection from becoming routine and predictable. Aries require activity, variety, and stimulation, but they are usually faithful to their relationship.

Because Aries men are prone to being Macho, they often find it difficult to get along with strong, independent women. But many Aries men are confident enough to know that a partner with character is important, and they give her the freedom and support she needs.

Aries women are known for being difficult to deal with. They are quite dictatorial, and many prefer a passive partner who lets them make the decisions. However, such relationships rarely continue since Aries women desire a powerful and confident mate who is on their level without overpowering them.

It's nothing! Those who break through the barrier will get a loyal, loving companion and partner whose joy in life will keep them going.

CHAPTER TWO

ARIES 2023 HOROSCOPE

Overview Aries 2023

This year, people born under the sign of Aries will be able to finish the projects they put off last year. Good luck will show up in your finances, career, love life, and health, according to your sun sign. Even though things will get better for you, you should be careful not to make mistakes that will make your life worse. You'll be happy because your relationships with other people will improve and you'll see the best in everything you do.

In this year, 2023, Jupiter would be in your sign until May, when it would move to the second house of Taurus, which is your second sign. This means that the focus will shift to family and money as the year goes on. Saturn would be moving through your 11th house of Aquarius, and in March, it will move into your 12th house of Pisces. This Saturn transit could make it hard for you to do spiritual things this year. Uranus goes through your second house of Taurus for the whole year, and Neptune goes through your twelfth house of Pisces.

Pluto would be in your tenth house of Capricorn, and in June, it would move to your eleventh house of Aquarius. These planetary patterns will have an effect on your money, love, family, career, and health in the coming year.

People with Aries birth signs would be able to pick up projects they had put on hold before. During the summer, Venus, the planet of love, would be in your fifth house of love. This would be a very good time. Couples should be careful, though, because there is a good chance that relationships will end. The movement of Jupiter and Uranus through your second house of finances would help you have a lot of money. This year, your health will be fine, and your social life will be at its best.

January 2023

Horoscope

A happy month is coming up, Aries. Jupiter in your sign brings you the good life, including trips to other countries, good food, good wine, and lots of other sensual pleasures. Your life is filled with a lot of hope. But you need to be more careful about your health, especially how much you weigh.

There is nothing seriously wrong with your health. It's just short-term stress caused by the short-term planets, and it will get better after the 20th. Since Mercury is in retrograde until the 17th, you should try to avoid medical tests or procedures if you can. Just hold off until after the 17th.

This month, life will move faster. Individual freedom is strong now and will get even stronger in the coming months. When Mars, the planet that rules your horoscope, moves forward on the 12th, you will know more about your own goals. This is an excellent month to make the changes you need to make to be happy in the future.

Even though love doesn't seem like a big deal anymore, single people can find love through their friends, groups, and professional and trade organizations. Friends can be cupid, or someone you thought of as a friend might want to be more than that. Dating can also happen through social media and online activities.

Overall, finance looks good, and it looks like your knowledge of technology is important. The high-tech and online worlds look like exciting opportunities for investors. You spend more on technology, which also helps you make more money. After Uranus moves forward on the 22nd, it will be easier to buy high-tech items.

Mars, which is in charge of your Horoscope, is "off limits" this month and will stay that way until May 4. So, you're "without boundaries" or outside your usual circle of friends, and it looks like you're having fun.

Love

The Mars-Venus trine is in effect from the 4th until the 27th of January. You have a way with words. Your charm draws others to you, which is amplified if there are affinities between you and them. To create and maintain a pleasant, open atmosphere, you need a feeling of purpose.

Those in a relationship are encouraged to shake things up a bit. While your partner may appreciate your efforts, don't go overboard! If you want your relationship to remain harmonious, you should accept your partner's preferences and aspirations.

Singles, this year is off to a great start. You never know who you'll run across in your social circles. Do not hurry the relationship if you want it to last.

Career

You will achieve your goals if you are patient and persistent. So quit placing so much pressure on yourself to get your brilliant ideas approved. The fact that not everyone is like you is a reminder to keep in mind. Your employer, coworkers, or customers require time to master new skills. So, be considerate and provide them with the space they need.

In terms of your career future, the prophecy from
the stars isn't all that encouraging. There is a good
chance that you and your superiors may disagree. You
must do all in your power to prevent this from
happening.

It's also possible that you'll be troubled with a sense
of uneasiness that will directly impact your work life.
You might try to make things right by making fast
career shifts or alterations to your company's
operations. This would be a really bad move. Any
adjustment should only be made after a thorough
examination of the situation. In addition, there would
be a lot of travel, although this also wouldn't be very
productive.

Finance

A prosperous month in terms of cash gain for you.
You might expect a bountiful crop of unexpected
rewards. Quite a number of you might also gain by
speculating. In addition, there is a considerable chance
that an elderly gentleman may do you a favor, which
could turn out to be a financial benefit.

Furthermore, you'll develop a way of dealing with
your superiors this month that will be quite
advantageous to your career. This has the potential to
be a significant benefit. Last but not least, a close

friendship with a number of intellectually and spiritually outstanding individuals will help you both monetarily and spiritually.

Health

This month, the stars are favoring your well-being, so you may expect to be healthy for most of the month. There would be a dramatic reduction in the frequency and severity of acute illnesses like fevers and inflammation. In most cases, they would not harm you in any way.

This also applies to those experiencing any type of dental issue. Denture problems should be taken seriously, although they have a strong possibility of being resolved. For your health, this is a good time, and those who are currently in good health may anticipate staying that way.

Travel

This is a terrific month to reap the benefits of travel, as the stars' prediction is highly positive on the matter. If you want to study or train in a foreign country, you have a good probability of this working well.

You'd prefer to travel by train, road, and air, with a substantial amount of air travel thrown in for good measure. A journey out of the country is a possibility as well. Only a portion of your travels will be for work. Whatever the case, you'll find what you're seeking on your journeys. The East direction is the best way to go if traveling.

Insights from the stars

Listen to the advice of someone with expertise and affection for you rather than letting go of the topic when the first difficulty or the least inconvenience emerges.

February 2023

Horoscope

This month, Jupiter in Aries and Mars in Gemini will always be there for you, providing you with a steady supply of energy and inspiration. Your morale is high in this positive environment. Ideas and initiatives are in good hands with you! You're chewing at the bit until the 11th since Mercury's inconsistency makes things difficult! With Mercury's transit to Aquarius, there are no more delays or obstructions. From the 12th, what was difficult becomes easy. Your sphere of influence expands to include fresh points of view and people who are receptive to your thoughts. Getting the funding you need to see your ideas through to completion is entirely within your grasp. From the 21st, you'll discover passion when it comes to love.

Love

It's not going to be a happy day till the 20th of this month. Venus, the planet of reflection, nudges you to do so. Instead of rushing things, take some time to think about what makes you happy and how you may incorporate it into your life. The arrival of Venus in your sign on the 21st brings you more self-confidence.

In a relationship, your actions build a gap. It's possible to get bored. Your words may have outstripped your ideas. Instead of adding fuel to the flames, think about how your spouse feels and what they are trying to say. Plan ahead of time to suit their needs.

If you're single, Venus is slowly undermining your sense of self-worth. It forces you to ponder your sexual prowess or the sentiments of the person you are seducing. There will be no more negative feelings on the 21st when Venus moves into Aries.

Career

You've got your ears to the ground. Many individuals come into your life. Every three seconds, you come up with a new concept, but until the eleventh, no one has agreed on it. Avoid being impatient since this will ensure that your ideas receive all the votes. Why? Why? Because you're at a good place in your life. February has the potential to be a fruitful month for you, but only if you exercise patience when the situation calls for it.

Finance

This month, your financial situation appears to be improving and might lead to long-term financial stability. You should expect to receive a bountiful harvest of unexpected financial rewards. Investing would bring in even more money for others, as would the market as a whole.

Health

Thanks to the blessings of Health Dame's fortune, you may anticipate to continue in good health for the foreseeable future. With regular care, people with long-term conditions like rheumatism and other symptoms like gas and wind in the digestive system will find significant alleviation from their symptoms. When it comes to teeth, this is also the case.

In addition, you should anticipate any predisposition to anxiousness to be alleviated and to cause significantly fewer problems than normal. A few flaws will be apparent, but these are readily remedied via regular exercise and a healthy diet. This is a good month for your health because there aren't any significant health risks.

Travel

The stars are smiling at you this month, so you may expect to make a lot of money while you're away. You'd largely take trains and roads, with some air travel thrown in. It is also possible that you will go outside the country.

Part of your travels would be work-related, while the remainder would be personal. However, regardless of the goal, you should be able to achieve it to the fullest extent possible. In addition to making new acquaintances, traveling is a great way to have a wonderful time. The East direction is the best way to go.

Insights from the stars

You're on a roll now! Nevertheless, keep in mind the emotions and sentiments of individuals in your immediate vicinity. Instead of wasting your time, you should invest it in a timely purpose.

March 2023

Horoscope

Jupiter's energies in Aries and Mars' in Gemini will expand your consciousness this month. You put all of your heart and soul into your endeavors. When you do what you enjoy, you're more likely to succeed. Your leadership qualities are further bolstered by Venus, Mercury, and the Sun, all currently transiting through the sign of Capricorn. This is a lucky month for you since you're experiencing a lot of good fortune.

On the 21st, a new Moon rises in your sign, giving you the motivation you need to take action. You take charge of your projects to ensure their success. On the other hand, events and circumstances will force you to examine all you've done. You'll make more money than you think if you don't hesitate.

Love

You're the drummer in your own band. You and your loved ones are in agreement. Everything is going swimmingly. Your charm has a way of enticing even the most skeptics. But if you don't want to face the music afterward, slow down and be more open.

There's a wall built between you and your significant other without your knowledge. Try to be more accessible. Pay attention to what your significant other has to say. If you do this, you won't have to worry about an impending disaster hanging over your head on the 26th!

Everything is OK if you're single when it comes to meeting new people! For the meetings to last, though, it's a lot more difficult! This conflict can only be solved if a genuine relationship is formed. Spend more time with the individual whose company you enjoy and whose thoughts and feelings you find fascinating.

Career

You're in luck till the 25th, so take advantage of it! You succeed because of your own efforts. Everybody admires you for your brilliant ideas. Then Mars loosens its grip on you since it's occupied with other people. Don't get down on yourself if things don't go according to your plan. You have all of the tools to restart them. How? You may start with simple improvements and work your way up.

Finance

A great month for your financial future. Unexpected gains would be a blessing to your bank account, and you would make a tidy profit from speculation. You would be able to get immediate and beneficial results from your work.

Travel

During this time of year, the stars are in your favor, and you'll reap the benefits of travel. This month, you'll travel for professional and personal reasons, respectively. For the most part, you'd take trains and roads, but you'd also take flights.

A journey out of the country is also a possibility. You'd be a huge success in all of this, and your business goals would be achieved. You'd also be able to have a relaxing vacation. The East direction is the best way to go.

Health

According to the stars, there is a lot of good news for your health this month. Toothaches of any sort should become much less uncomfortable. Be careful not to overwork yourself since this may easily disrupt a good mood; create a new routine that doesn't put too much strain on yourself.

You cannot afford to take any shortcuts or risks with your health. Everything else is OK. Those who are already prone to anxiety would not be bothered by an increase in their risk. When it comes to health, this month is a good one to avoid any significant issues.

Insights from the stars

It's fantastic to see that you're moving forward. Be careful to build relationships with your partners, new acquaintances, and loved ones. You will avoid disappointment if you follow this advice.

-

April 2023

Horoscope

As Jupiter is in your sign in April, it stimulates and fosters your progress in both personal and financial matters. Improving your life or making yourself better. It boosts your self-esteem and your ability to think creatively. You'll be pushed to take action by Jupiter. It opens up new options for you, which fits well with your multitasking tendencies. A more practical energy is urging you this month to look at the financial viability of your plans and objectives.

The dissonances caused by Mars in Cancer should be taken into consideration by looking at external factors. Instead of going all out to win, try to come to an agreement with these responsibilities. Take a look at your finances before you start and be more frugal than usual.

Love

You'll have less room to move until the 12th. Getting that flame going is hard! Having a "win-at-all-costs" attitude doesn't get you what you want. Since Venus is in Gemini, everything works out in the end. Your relationships are fun to be a part of because they are lighthearted.

It is normal for people in a relationship to have different personalities. Mars makes this effect in Cancer's dissonances even stronger. From the 12th, you'll be able to get back together with your partner, who will be more willing to see the good things about your relationship.

Even though your charm makes people notice you, it's still hard to be single. You can be sure that your sex appeal can't be denied. On the 12th, Venus will be in Gemini, which will help you find your way. The unexpected knows how to do what it does best.

Career

It's a success because you're a really creative person. You know how to take chances when you need to, and it's this that propels you to success. You've been outpacing the rest of the pack for some time now. As a result, your good fortune has been boosted. It is in your best interest, and you are correct. For Aries, luck is a good thing, but if your initiatives are going to last, you need to do the math. For the time being, temper your aspirations a bit.

Finance

According to your sun sign, this is not a good month for your financial future. There's a good chance your relationships with your superiors will deteriorate to the point where you'll be forced to take a hit financially. As a result, you must be on the lookout for such a scenario and prepare ahead of time in order to avoid it.

You may not be able to meet your goals if there is a lack of opportunity. It's also possible to focus too much on making unreported cash. Everything in your life will suffer as a result of this. Avoiding unnecessary investments is also important.

Health

During this month, the stars will bestow upon your health and prosperity. Those prone to clammy hands and feet may notice a marked improvement in their health during this month.

If you're dealing with a long-term dental issue, you'll be less bothered and more likely to get cured if you take it seriously. The fact that anxiousness and related problems would be much reduced is also a source of comfort. You are unlikely to encounter any significant health issues in the foreseeable future.

Travel

This is a great month for reaping the rewards of travel, as the horoscopes are quite promising. It's possible that some of you may take pilgrimages to holy sites that will serve as a lasting reminder of your experiences.

Higher education or training in a foreign country would go as planned for anyone who chooses to do so. Traveling for business would be a huge success. You'd primarily travel by train or car, with some air travel thrown in for good measure. It is also feasible to take a trip overseas. The East direction is the best way to go.

Insights from the stars

Instead of retaliating, take a step back and evaluate what's causing the problems. There's a good chance that you'll benefit from this.

May 2023

Horoscope

Jupiter's good influences have been helping you for a few months now. It gives you the chance to rethink your everyday routine or start over with new ideas. After a few days in Aries, he'll be leaving. The month of May is the best time to make use of the lucky star and evolution's many resources.

Make the most of the chances that come your way by taking advantage of them. But to make them real, it will be necessary for you to work out your commitments imposed by the Cancerian energy that you are born into. It's important to remember that the feeling of being squandered will pass.

Your business will be handled by Leo starting March 20th. Even though it appeared to be jeopardized before, it will be completed under the present ideal circumstances.

Love

Until the 7th, everything will be fine. Then things get complicated! The spark of desire that had been rekindled a few weeks ago has gone out again. How? By putting you in situations where you can't get out of them on your own.

To those in committed relationships: Congratulations! You've been busy for a while. Your relationship needs to calm down this month and return to a regular schedule. Soothe yourself instead of pushing things. That special someone will shower you with love and appreciation.

In the case of those who are single, When Venus is in Gemini, your romantic relationships progress in a laid-back and diverting environment. The 7th brings Venus into Cancer, which causes a flurry of restrictions to arise! To keep a relationship going, you need to be willing to make certain compromises.

Career

Taking advantage of Jupiter in Aries' tremendous opportunities and passion is best done now. Take advantage of each opportunity that comes your way.

After that, you'll be able to put your life back together. There's no need to panic if you're having trouble getting started or if you've already begun but are having difficulty moving forward. It's better to compromise and get what you want than waste time.

On the 17th, Jupiter turns its attention to the financial sector. If you're a little more cautious than usual, luck will come your way.

Finance

This month's horoscope predicts that you'll have a good month financially. This month, you're more likely to have arguments with your superiors, which puts you and them at odds, but by the middle of the month, you'll be able to work things out, which will lead to a significant gain.

To avoid substantial losses, stay away from any investment activities that aren't absolutely required. It's best to avoid all forms of gambling altogether. However, the current economic situation is not conducive to making investments or creating new businesses. Such preparations should be put on hold for the foreseeable future.

Health

This month, the gods are on your side when it comes to your health, and it is highly probable that you will avoid any significant health issues this month. A quick spell of acute sickness, such as a fever or inflammation, would be alleviated, and these issues would no longer be a major concern for you. Such a respite is possible this month since it is a good one.

However, there are reasons to be wary about one's oral health. This might lead to dental issues if you're not careful. Bone injuries, which are highly uncommon this month, should also be treated cautiously.

Travel

The stars aren't exactly aligned to make this a great month to travel, so you won't get much out of it. During your travels, there is a chance that you will be hurt or have a physical problem. As a result, you should proceed with caution and only take little chances.

You'd like to travel alone and primarily by rail or road, with some air travel thrown in for good measure. Traveling for work or business purposes may account for a portion of your journeys. It's safe to say that they would be a waste of time. The possibility of a trip abroad is not ruled out. The best way to go is east.

Insights from the stars

Don't dwell on the negative aspects of your life if you want them to go away. Also, don't be too self-reliant.

June 2023

Horoscope

Thanks to the Leo and Gemini energy flowing through you, you'll be able to take advantage of Jupiter's possibilities while he's in Aries this month. Mars encourages you to set lofty goals and reach for the sky this month. Taking action and making choices are emphasized. Natural leadership comes from inside so dissonant energies in Cancer will compel you to fulfill duties you were unaware of between January 1st and April 4th, as well as starting on or after January 22nd. Seeing things as inescapable will not help you organize your responsibilities. If you don't have the same sense of risk, aid people who don't have it.

Be a calming influence on others around you even while feeling frazzled. Considering the long term will also help you financially.

Love

You have a great deal of stamina! You're more concerned about how you look than you were before.

Your magnetic personality makes you stand out. You make others want to be jealous. We all face the same challenges regardless of whether dating or not! You retake power over your loved ones so that they may learn about this obsession that captivates you, and you do this so that they can share in your joy.

Your imagination may run wild between the twelfth and the twenty-seventh if you are currently in a love relationship. Your relationship will be free of the routine that makes it tough to sustain. It is advisable to take a short vacation from your relationship.

As long as you're single, there's no need to give in to the demands of your partner. You're in charge here, so do anything you want! This month's gathering is expected to be nice and informal. After then, it's up to you!

Career

In addition to the Gemini energies that inspire you, Mars in Leo has a huge impact on your success! It offers you a certain magnetism that attracts others who will help you in your endeavors. Some people will succumb to your charms, which you will exploit without restraint. Be careful not to overlook these minor things while using your magic. In what way? In terms of your financial well-being!

Finance

What the stars say about your financial situation this month paints a bleak picture. You've been asked to investigate this side of things, which aren't quite as flashy. To combat this, lower your sails and demonstrate that you're taking things seriously. Your desires will be fulfilled by doing so.

There's a good chance you'll have a bad relationship with your bosses if the company faces significant losses. You can avoid this if you plan ahead and take proactive measures.

Gambling should be avoided at all costs.

Health

As a result of the favorable conditions, your health should be improving this month. Those inclined to chronic conditions like rheumatism and digestive abnormalities like gas and excess wind in the digestive tract will see a considerable improvement. As a result, taking even the most basic precautions should keep you safe from such issues.

However, you should use caution if you have a prolonged sore throat. Complications should be thoroughly identified and addressed without delay. This might have a negative impact on a healthy and positive body system if it is not done. You have nothing else to worry about other than this.

Travel

Given the omens' unfavorable outlook, it may be tough to reap the benefits of travel this month. Performing artists, including singers, painters, dancers, and others, may not be as creative while traveling. Some of them may even suffer a setback as a result of this.

For the most part, you'd want to travel by train or car, with a significant amount of air travel.

Foreign travel isn't out of the question. Despite the fact that most of this would be related to your career or business, it is almost probable that the expected outcomes would not be met. The most advantageous direction is South.

Insights from the stars

If you put your mind to it, you can accomplish your goals. If you want the magic to work, you can't be irritated by folks who take their time. The best thing you can do for them is to reassure them.

July 2023

Horoscope

As Venus continues her stay in Leo this July, you're more focused on your own needs and desires than ever before. You're looking forward to a fun time. Because of this, it is out of the question for you to suffer in the blazing summer heat. If you want to alter your mind, then you'll do it. The shift from Mercury to Leo opens up many new ways to have fun, and these energy revives your friendships.

This month will be filled with many fun activities and lovely get-togethers. But there are other less joyous emotions in circulation. However, despite your best efforts, it is possible that you may have to deal with a few minor issues.

Love

In recent weeks, there have been fewer seizures or other difficulties. In any case, it's possible that you've come to some sort of decision. If you're single this month, you've got a lot riding on the quality of the relationships your in. In Leo, you'll be able to accomplish your ambitions.

Avoid the "all or nothing" mindset this month if you're in a relationship, as it might lead to long periods of quiet and a crisis of possessiveness. Keep your cool and reassure your significant other that you care by making passionate declarations of your love.

If you're single, this is a great time to meet someone new! Venus is doing an excellent job introducing you to someone very special this month. If you want the magic to work, you must have faith in your sex appeal and be romantic when appropriate.

Career

Despite the fact that you're working on other, more exciting endeavors, a string of unfortunate occurrences has forced you to focus on your present business. You, Aries, seem to be thinking of something else. As a result, you might end up paying the price for not paying attention to these minor issues! So, if you don't want to find yourself in a predicament, you need to think hard. As a result, the projects you're working on will progress in a way that benefits you.

Moreover, you'll be plagued by anxiety for the duration of the month. Your entire professional behavior would be affected. If you're prone to mood swings and are considering making a career or company move, you should do so only after careful consideration. Chances are that despite your efforts, the accomplishments you had in mind would not be realized.

When it comes to money, this industry pulls you back to reality. Unfortunately, you may not be able to use it. In contrast, if you're practical, you'll swiftly bounce back.

Finance

According to the stars, you'll have a gloomy outlook on your financial future. Writers, poets, and others of their kind should stock up on supplies for the rainy day since they are likely to experience a dry period this month.

Risky behavior may have resulted in significant losses for some of you. Avoid all forms of gambling, big or small. It's also possible that your relationships with your superiors may deteriorate to the point where you suffer significant losses. You may avoid this by taking some proactive measures in advance.

Health

The constellations aligned with you this month are highly beneficial to your health. Those with a sensitive chest or lungs and susceptible to chest and pulmonary diseases would likely benefit significantly from the blessings of this month. Overwork can lead to weariness and subsequent sluggishness.

You can easily avoid this if you don't put in too much effort. Everything will be OK after this is completed. This might also assist you in overcoming the potential of some types of nervous system diseases, however, this is a remote possibility. If you take good care of yourself this month, you may expect to be in peak physical condition. The health of your teeth should be given more attention.

Travel

There isn't much to be gained by travel based on the predictions of the stars. Traveling as a writer, poet, or other creative person isn't always easy. In fact, some might be significantly affected by the ineffectiveness of their stay.

The majority of your journey would be via train or road, with some air travel thrown in. The possibility of a trip abroad is not ruled out. In the real world, these efforts are quite unlikely to even result in a holiday, which is unfortunate. The best way to go is East.

Insights from the stars

This month has been a good one for your loved ones! You should definitely enjoy it! But if you want to go farther, you must respond positively to their sensitive expectations.

August 2023

Horoscope

Venus and the Sun in Leo will always be there to support your growth this month. It's a bit of a bummer when Venus goes retrograde, since you won't be able to get what you want quite as fast. An expectation that your impatience cannot bear will be placed upon you. To take benefit of these disadvantages, you must consent. The retrograde of Venus helps you to discover what you truly desire. This Venusian retrograde will also allow you to get up to speed if you've missed anything or someone. If you ease your renowned desire, the transfer of Mars to Libra, which is expected on the 28th, will be simpler.

Love

Venus is erratic and difficult to please. As you relax, your senses are sharpened at the same time. Despite your best efforts, you have no control over the people you care about. Get it by playing the game! Although it is not clear at the moment, you will not regret it.

Certainties crumble under the pressure of the passage of time. The feeling of excitement is no longer present at all. Do not think of these annoyances as a matter of mortality because they are only passengers in your life. But if you're in a relationship, you can use it to your advantage by finding out about your partner's needs and goals, even if they differ from yours.

However, if you are in a relationship, you have the opportunity to take advantage of it by learning about your partner's wants and objectives, even if they are different from your own. You can do this even if the two of you have very different goals in life.

A narrow, vacant corridor separates the couples from the singles. Do not be startled if you feel overwhelmed by uncertainty this month. Now is a wonderful moment to take a fresh look at your methods. The most effective way to convey your emotions is via reflection.

Career

Even though this month is ideal for vacations and recovery, the stars demand that you maintain a strict watch on your activities. On the worst days, a happy and last-minute event might be delayed! Because inconveniences seldom happen in a vacuum, unforeseen financial circumstances may compel you to accept a compromise by pushing back your deadlines.

This solution will assist you in resolving a difficult situation, despite its unappealing nature. This industry's financial health may be in jeopardy.

Finance

In terms of your financial future, the stars' predictions aren't all that encouraging. You may suffer significant losses as a result of investing. As a result, you should avoid all forms of investments. Negative feelings against your supervisors or coworkers will almost certainly result in major financial setbacks. But don't worry; they'll calm down once you figure out where they're coming from.

You may, however, avoid this by putting in the effort and preparing ahead. You may put so much emphasis on not making money that you don't know where it came from or getting into shady deals. This is not in your best interest and might get you into trouble. Investing or starting a new business would likewise be difficult because of the current atmosphere.

Health

Maintaining a healthy lifestyle is easier this month because of the favorable alignment of the stars in your favor. The likelihood of having a stomach or other digestive organs that are easily upset is significantly reduced. Coughs, colds, and asthma, which are all common disorders of the chest, will be eliminated.

With good dental care, you can ensure that nothing bad occurs to your teeth because there is a cause to be concerned about the condition of your teeth. It's possible that you're easily agitated and have a little disturbed state of mind, as well. Maintaining excellent mental and physical health may be as simple as remaining calm and balanced.

Travel

As the stars indicate, this month's horoscope does not bode well for anyone looking to make money on the road. This month, you're more likely to travel alone, mainly by car or train, with some flights tossed in for good measure.

In addition, you may have to go overseas for a job or pleasure. Because of this certainty, these efforts are unlikely to produce the promised earnings or deliver the expected joy and satisfaction. East would be the most ideal direction.

Insights from the stars

If the others withdraw slightly, it's because they feel the need to collect their thoughts first. Do precisely the same. It'll be more beneficial in the long run than taking up arms against the heavens themselves.

September 2023

Horoscope

Your ability to deal with Mars in Libra's onslaught will determine whether or not you have a successful autumn season. Antagonism against your sign might have unexpected and even violent consequences because of the opposition it inspires.

Events and circumstances this month force you to make decisions that might lead you into an undesirable scenario. Avoid making decisions based on your emotions if you want things to go nicely. Avoid using anger as a means of resolving your issues.

Take some cues from Venus in Leo to keep your cool and make the most of Mars's Libra energy. Its retrograde provides the impression that nothing is progressing. Taking a direct stroll from the 16th re-establishes your good energy.

Love

Although there is still a significant amount of work to be done, the situation is becoming more transparent. You have until the 16th of this month to give some thought to your goals and objectives. Because of this, it's a good idea to be on the lookout for indications that there could be friction in your relationship. Mars is one of your ruling planets because it makes you want to make a commitment when you see something beautiful. Make an effort this month to accept a future with your spouse rather than dismissing the possibility of one together.

If you're in a relationship, you must be experiencing an amazing amount of love. You are prepared for everything that may occur between you and your sweetheart, regardless of the circumstances. Then comes the beginning of the unpleasantness. It's almost certain that you and your partner will part ways. Put some restraint on your zeal. Wait a moment before continuing to speak. Why? Because what you're doing is not acceptable in this context.

Singles who are actively looking for a romantic partner and have recently found themselves in a relationship rut should not lose hope; the dry spell will eventually end. You can find joy in the little things that life has to offer. Be careful with your words since they have the potential to get ahead of your ideas and ruin a potentially beautiful romance.

Career

Aries! The more irritated you become about the initial delay, the more likely you will have a breakdown. Your brand's reputation will be tarnished as an added benefit. Slow down, even if it's not your style. Please don't be frustrated with those who require additional time to complete tasks. Do not act on impulse while you are at it. The consequences of a contract breach should be considered carefully.

There's a good chance you'll disagree with your bosses. You should do all in your power to avoid such a situation because the consequences would be terrible for your professional future.

Finance

The stars predict that this month's events will not be favorable for your financial progress. Some of you may lose significant money if you speculate on the stock market. To avoid any kind of investment, then, it is best to avoid it at all costs.

There are also signs that any disagreement or litigation you would be involved in would probably be resolved against you, resulting in significant damages. As a result, you must make every effort to postpone any such choice until a more favorable time. Negative feelings toward superiors or coworkers are also likely to develop; avoid this if at all possible to avoid large financial losses. This month's financial outlook is gloomy. So tune in and get right to the point. In this way, you can avoid making a mistake.

Health

When the stars align in your favor, it's an excellent month to be a health freak this month. This month would alleviate short-lived acute illnesses including fevers and inflammations. In all likelihood, you would not be bothered by any of this. Back pain would be alleviated in the same way.

There are, however, reasons to be concerned about an eye infection. While this may cause some discomfort, it may be avoided by taking the proper precautions, such as cleaning up after yourself and taking preventative medicine. Your health has improved significantly in just one month, which is encouraging news.

Travel

As far as benefits from travels are concerned, the prophecy from the stars is not encouraging. For the most part, you'll be on the road or train this month, with some flights thrown in for good measure.

A trip abroad is also a possibility. No matter how hard you work, you can be confident that none of your efforts will pay off in terms of financial gain or personal fulfillment. Unfortunately, this is a real depiction of the situation. It's possible that most of your trip is pointless and could be done without. The West is the best direction.

Insights from the stars

Having too much energy might cause you to do things you don't intend. As a result, instead of getting caught up in endless arguments, try to identify compromises everyone can agree with.

October 2023

Horoscope

The pressure is on you through the medium of Mars until the 12th and until the 22nd through the Sun and Mercury. The Libran energies force you to take a stride forward and then a step backward. You'll be difficult to follow and grasp as a result of this. On the other hand, if you agree, you may go about it in another way. How? With your family, friends, or coworkers by demonstrating mutual respect for one another. This may seem like a waste of effort, but it will protect you from bad outcomes.

If you are unable to listen to the needs of others, you will not achieve your full potential. Your situational analysis also plays a role in the decision-making process. You'll need to calm your infamous impatience to get the most out of this small gem.

Love

Until the 9th, Venus in Leo will keep things harmonious in your relationships. Mercury, however, takes a backseat when it comes to making commitments or expressing your future plans. Consequently, what you say determines the course of your romantic relationships. Be mindful of what you're about to say before you do.

If you're in a relationship, you're especially concerned about Libra's energy. In a situation like this, it's important to keep your beliefs in check. It's important to discover and respect your partner's strengths in order to restore calm.

Until September 9th, Venus promotes meeting new people through fun activities such as going out or watching a movie for single people. Then, it creates seductive links through your employment or other hobbies. Be patient and on time if you want magic to work for you.

Career

Aries, if you want things to move well this month, you'll have to do it yourself! Slow down your maniacal enthusiasm and impatience. Make sure you take into account what other people have to say. If you must say something, speak in a less direct manner. Don't lay the responsibility at the feet of others. Make sure to focus on their strengths and devotion. If you do this, your popularity will soar rather than sink one more notch.

Health

This month, you have a favorable collection of circumstances promoting excellent health. Chronic diseases like rheumatism and gout, as well as digestive system abnormalities like gas and an excess of wind, would be greatly reduced. It's important to remember that this does not give you the green light to abandon all prudence.

You have good reason to be concerned about the status of your oral health. If you take good care of your teeth, you can assure that nothing bad happens. As a result, you have a month in which you will not have to deal with any severe health threats.

Travel

There would be a lot of traveling, which would be quite advantageous. South would be the most beneficial direction to travel. There is a good chance that you'll have to relocate, whether for professional or personal reasons. Decide carefully before making any changes because a hasty move might erase all of your hard work thus far.

For the most part, you'd like to travel alone, either by car or train, with a decent amount of air travel. The possibility of a journey abroad cannot be ruled out. South is the best direction.

Finances

It's not looking good for you financially this month, according to the stars. Jupiter has your best interests at heart. Listen to his advice, even if you think it's too cautious if you want him to give you the best. Consider the long-term consequences of your actions.

First, your working relationships with your superiors may turn for the worst. As a result, significant losses may likely occur. As a result, you must take preventative measures in the early stages of the situation.

Insights from the stars

You'll be fooled by the Libran vibes. Use common sense, even if it bores you, to stay clear of these hassles.

November 2023

Horoscope

You have been through some tough months, yet you've remained fair. Nothing can shake your resolve. Staying calm is something you have to do for yourself when necessary. However, this does not mean that you won't be able to find the time and feel bored at some point. Movement returns to your life as a result of the Venus transit through Libra on the 9th. Fresh air is sent to you on the 11th as Mercury moves through Sagittarius.

This month's astrological forecast gives you chances to reframe your mindset instead of making dramatic adjustments. For the greatest possible outcome, avoid creating confrontation in order to obtain your independence since this would lead you down the wrong path. Instead, practice polite negotiation skills.

Love

After the 8th, you put out the effort. You project a professional picture of yourself. Control your legendary enthusiasm, and you'll reap the rewards. As Venus moves into Libra, things begin to shift. As a result of the tremendous gift of passion you have in your relationships, you'll always be a struggle to follow.

Because Venus is in Libra, you're worried about it. You should be aware of your reactions if you're in a relationship in this situation. You'll be able to preserve the peace if you and your spouse stay diplomatic and affectionate. In contrast, when you stand up for nothing, things are different.

If you're single, you're able to form bonds with individuals who are kind and positive. If you're in this situation, everything is conceivable. Your search for love can end here. Keep a tight rein on your fabled zeal if you want this miracle to last.

Career

Working in a team is a stressful experience, and taking control of the company's day-to-day operations. Despite the fact that this strategy has been working out well for you, this month, it may pull a trick on you.

Always avoid offering directions, Aries, especially if you want to keep your high popularity rating! Think about other people's decisions before trying to overrule them. Instead, share your thoughts with the world because they are awesome.

Finance

Your financial situation is looking up this month thanks to a favorable alignment of the stars in your natal chart. Your business acumen has been on full display this month! Now is the perfect time to trust your instincts and make money. Investors might expect to do well this month if they stick with it. As a result, you may increase business revenues due to improved connections with your superiors.

When it comes to making investments or establishing initiatives, the atmosphere is favorable. As a result, such strategies should be implemented.

Health

The constellations aligned with you this month are particularly supportive of good health. We merely need to provide a word of warning about going too hard too soon. By preventing this and spreading energy smartly, normal operations can keep going without putting too much stress on the system.

The easiest way to do this is to make a whole new schedule of things to do. Maintaining optimum oral health and taking all necessary precautions is also a good idea. From a health standpoint, this month is quite positive.

Travel

This month, you should be able to make a lot of money by traveling, since the stars favor this. Traveling can be energizing and inspiring for artists of all kinds, whether they're painters, musicians, or writers. The amount of time spent on the road would also be highly useful.

Traveling alone is more common this month, with most of your trips taking place by car, train, and plane. You can't rule out a vacation overseas. Whatever your purpose, whether to do business or simply have a relaxing vacation, you'd have a great time doing it. The West is the best direction.

Insights from the stars

The vastness of the universe invites you to revise your preconceptions and assumptions. Keep your accomplishments instead of destroying them in the name of your beloved freedom.

December 2023

Horoscope

This month, Mars in Sagittarius is your best bet for reinvigorating yourself. And Mercury and the Sun, which are both in this sign, add to the effect. With the help of these energies, you're able to achieve your goals with confidence and good fortune. By knowing who you are, you can take back control of the wheel of life.

Dissonances emanating from Capricorn will bring you bad luck despite your fierce will. Do not take them as a personal attack because they are not meant to make you miserable. These risks are designed to keep you from making judgments that might trap you in a deadlock that would be difficult to break out of.

Love

There are excellent moments and periods of doubt until the 4th of this month, when Venus is in Libra. Finally, the tone shifts to Scorpio. Keep your relationships out of the abyss by not taking risks with

them that might lead to irreparable harm. Why?
Their chances of getting out unhurt would be slim.

For those in a partnership, even if Venus in Libra
causes problems, she does not jeopardize your
relationship. From the fifth day of her stay in Scorpio,
you may find yourself in an impossible scenario. Play
it safe this month.

In the case of those who are single, Venus in Libra
may have helped you come to terms with the idea of
committing to someone. For those who aren't interested
in getting married on their vacation, there is a whole
other level of excitement awaiting you.

Career

Victory and accomplishments provide you with
wings. You're right to want to go further since having
a can-do attitude is conducive to pushing the envelope
of what is achievable. You have the audacity to do so.
You aren't afraid to try new things. Why? Because you
want to fight and to do it better than the others. If you
don't want to be broken by your desires, be careful not
to go overboard.

Finance

Your financial future is in jeopardy this month due to a slew of bad luck stars. There are positive and encouraging influxes to this region from Jupiter's Taurus position. Some of you will suffer losses due to your speculative activities; that is clear. As a result, it's best to avoid all forms of gambling, including online ones.

Furthermore, there are reasons to believe that you'll be prone to conflict with your coworkers or your employees if you are a business owner, which might lead to severe consequences regarding profit. The good news is that you can strive to avoid this. Taking the necessary steps in advance might help you avoid this situation. It's not a good time to start new initiatives or make investments. As a result, be cautious not to put yourself in unnecessary danger.

Health

As a result of excellent conditions, you should not be concerned about your health during this period. This month would greatly alleviate predispositions to persistent colds and mucus overflow. With the right treatment and care, people with a condition called hemorrhoids can expect a better quality of life.

Despite this, it's important to remember to take care of your teeth as well as your body as a whole! When it comes to this, any lapses in your physical health might have serious consequences. You may expect to be healthy this month, which is a nice one overall.

Travel

This is not a good month for travel: this is a month where you may lose a lot of money since the stars are not in your favor. If you're going on a trip, there's a chance that something may go wrong. Avoid unnecessary risks by being cautious.

You'd primarily travel by road and train, with a small amount of air travel thrown in for good measure. The possibility of overseas travel is not ruled out. These vacations might be a waste of time in every aspect. You would not be satisfied with it. It's best to head East if you can.

Insights from the stars

Be as flexible as you like with your ideas. You shouldn't second-guess your accomplishments, either. Why? This is because the choices that are presented to you are only available for a limited amount of time.

Printed in Great Britain
by Amazon

14700287R00047